Original title:
The Resilient Oak

Editor: Jessica Elisabeth Luik
Author: Luise Luik
ISBN HARDBACK: 978-9916-86-341-1
ISBN PAPERBACK: 978-9916-86-342-8

Endless Vigil

The night is dark, the stars are still,
A watchful eye on every hill.
Whispers float in evening's chill,
Through woods, the tales entwined fulfill.

Guardians stand in shadows deep,
Their promises to nature keep.
While mortals drift to boundless sleep,
In vigil's quiet, secrets seep.

Oft forgotten, silent soldier,
Standing firm, growing older.
Beyond the grasp of twilight's holder,
An ageless sentinel, ever bolder.

Earth’s Wooden Sentinel

Among the greens of valleys wide,
A stalwart figure does abide.
Secrets whispered, branches sighed,
Ancient tales within them glide.

Roots that delve through earth so deep,
Where memories of ages seep.
Standing tall where shadows creep,
A sentinel's eternal keep.

Leaves that dance with gentle breeze,
Silent witness through the trees.
Life’s old stories carried free,
By the wooden guardian's decree.

Wind-Swept Monarch

In the forest, proud and tall,
A monarch hears the wind's call.
Branches sway, a leafy shawl,
Nature's whispers gently fall.

Crowned with leaves of emerald hue,
Waving in the sky so blue.
Harkening the old and new,
Timeless tales the winds imbue.

Roots embrac the earth so fast,
Memories of an ancient past.
In the breeze, a shadow cast,
Monarch whispering to the last.

Silent Echo of Ages

By the rivers, timeless streams,
Mysteries dwell where sunlight beams.
In the forest, ancient dreams,
Silent echo often redeems.

Etched in bark, sagas told,
Tales of wisdom, brave and bold.
Through the seasons, warmth and cold,
Echoes of the ages unfold.

Lush canopies where whispers weave,
Underneath, the hearts that grieve.
Branches cradled, lives reprieve,
In their shade, old souls believe.

Tranquil and Unbowed

In whispers of the morning light,
Nature speaks in calm refrain.
Dew-kissed leaves in dawn's clear sight,
Find peace in each day's gain.

Among the shadows, soft and mild,
Dreams awaken, hearts unbowed.
Light imbues the forest wild,
In serenity, we're enshroud.

Winds hum softly through the boughs,
Silver streams reflect the sky.
Unyielding stands the ancient vows,
Of earth's eternal, gentle sigh.

Roots That Bind the Earth

Hidden veins beneath the soil,
Whisper tales of strength and life.
Ancient roots that never toil,
Stand firm against the strife.

Fingers reaching, deep they spread,
Cradling earth in tight embrace.
Bound by bonds unseen, unsaid,
Forever in their place.

Life springs forth from anchored hearts,
Roots that bind, yet set us free.
Earth's enduring work of arts,
In their veins, our legacy.

Tides of Change in Timber

Seasons shift with whispered grace,
Leaves transform in silent waves.
Cycles woven into place,
In their dance, our forests saves.

Colors swirl in autumn's breeze,
Timber's testament to time.
Ebb and flow through ageless trees,
Nature's rhythm, pure and prime.

Change is written in each ring,
Stories of a life well-told.
As each season gifts its sting,
Roots remain, though branches fold.

Woodland Watcher

Stalwart stands the ancient oak,
Guardian of woodland's dream.
Into shadows, softly spoke,
Held secure by nature's seam.

Eyes that see the passing years,
Whisper of the ages gone.
Silent witness, of joys, of tears,
At dusk, at dawn, till life is done.

Through the boughs, the watcher stands,
Keeper of the forest's heart.
In its shade, all creatures' lands,
Together, yet apart.

Woodland Witness

In the shadows of ancient trees,
A tale of time softly weaves.
Whispering winds the leaves caress,
Nature's secrets they confess.

Amidst the rustle, a witness stands,
Silent guardian of these lands.
Birdsong echoes, pure and true,
Every dawn feels fresh and new.

Moonlight dances on the moss,
Every path a choice to cross.
In twilight's embrace, truths unfurl,
Untouched by the rush of the world.

Deep roots anchor stories old,
In every whisper, legends told.
The woodland holds its mysteries dear,
Echoes of the past linger near.

Brave Guardian of the Woods

Among the towering pines so tall,
A sentinel of the forest calls.
Eyes ablaze with ancient might,
Protector of the day and night.

Silent steps through brush and fern,
Lessons of the wild to learn.
Claws and fangs, courage bright,
A defender unseen in twilight.

Through storm and sun, steadfast stand,
Heart of the forest in your hand.
Guardian fierce, spirit free,
Soul entwined with every tree.

Breath of earth and sky you keep,
In shadows deep, your vigil steep.
A constant force in green embrace,
Keeper of this sacred space.

Soul of the Ancestral Tree

Ancient branches touch the sky,
Rooted deep where secrets lie.
Leaves whisper tales born of old,
Stories timeless, yet untold.

Through seasons' dance, strength prevails,
In every breeze, an epic tale.
Sun and rain, frost and thaw,
Nature's law without a flaw.

Generations in each ring,
Silent limbs in solace sing.
Legacy of green and grow,
Wisdom in the peaceful flow.

Eternal spirit of the wood,
Bearer of the past so good.
In shade and light, history,
Soul of the tree, forever free.

Nature's Pillar

Majestic oak beneath the sky,
A pillar strong where birds fly.
With arms wide spread in leafy cheer,
Foundation of the wild is clear.

Roots delve deep in earthen bed,
Silent strength where life is fed.
From soil to sun, energy flows,
In every branch, life bestows.

Seasons turn, yet stand you tall,
Witness to the forest's call.
In sunlight's gold and moon's embrace,
Nature's rhythm you trace.

Timeless giant of the green,
Keeper of all that's seen.
With steadfast grace, life endures,
Nature's pillar, ever pure.

Life Through Rough Winters

In the stillness of a frozen dawn,
Whispers of warmth are but a dream,
Yet deep beneath the snow and frost,
Life stirs in an unseen stream.

Branches creak in the silence,
Roots speak secrets down below,
For even in the harshest chill,
Hope finds a way to grow.

Shadows dance in fleeting light,
Crystals glint on ice-clad bough,
A stubborn will to persevere,
Lies beneath the frigid plow.

Keeper of Secrets

Beneath the twilight's watchful eye,
A silent oath, a whispered sigh,
In shadowed nooks where echoes lie,
The keeper guards the passerby.

Ancient walls that tell no tale,
Silent mirth and solemn wail,
Within the chambers, dark and pale,
Secrets dwell, quiet and frail.

Veiled behind an unseen veil,
A trust bestowed, never to fail,
With steadfast heart, they never quail,
Guardians of the whispered trail.

Strength Beneath the Bark

Mighty oak and slender pine,
In their depths, true strength does shine,
Beneath the bark, a tale untold,
Of silent battles, fierce and bold.

The seasons test their noble grace,
Wind and rain their forms embrace,
Yet stand they do in steadfast march,
With strength beneath their rugged arch.

The rings that mark their hidden past,
Record of time forever cast,
In nature’s book of life, they spark,
A testament to strength beneath the bark.

Echoes of Tenacity

In the valley of forgotten dreams,
Where hope is but a fleeting gleam,
Echoes of tenacity arise,
A steadfast spirit in disguise.

From shadows dark and voices still,
A force emerges, iron will,
To challenge fate, defy despair,
With courage lit by boundless flare.

Through trials bleak and nights unkind,
The echoes leave no soul behind,
Their song a guide to hearts that seek,
Strength found within the meek.

A Sentinel's Tale

In the hush of night, he stands alone,
Unafraid of shadows, flesh, or bone.
His eyes see far, his heart beats clear,
Through every trial, he knows no fear.

The winds may howl, the wolves may howl,
Yet steadfast stays his noble soul.
Guarding secrets that time forgot,
A sentinel, fate's unyielding knot.

His armor gleams in moonlight's glow,
A silent watcher, friend or foe?
From ages past to future's veil,
He guards the night, a timeless tale.

Through victory and through sorrow's song,
Beside his post, he's ever strong.
A beacon in the darkest night,
A sentinel of endless light.

Survival Amidst Chaos

In lands where wildfires blaze and grow,
Where rivers twist in torrid flow,
We find our strength in every fight,
Survival is our guiding light.

Amongst the ruins, we reclaim,
Our spirits kin to untamed flame.
Through chaos, we carve through the strife,
Resilient hearts, embracing life.

Surrounded by both fear and dread,
We forward march, despite the spread.
Our bodies ache, our minds remain,
Resilience forged in every pain.

Amidst the storm, we build anew,
Our roots hold fast as changes brew.
Survivors rise, with hope we cope,
In chaos thrives our highest hope.

In the Wake of Storms

When tempests roar and torrents rise,
And thunderous echoes split the skies,
We find our strength, our courage born
In every drop, from dusk till dawn.

The wreckage left in storm's cruel path,
May kindle sorrow, stoke our wrath.
But in the wake, we stand as one,
Our battles fought, yet not undone.

The clouds shall part, reveal the sun,
In fields where tears and rain did run.
Each storm a test, each gale a guide,
New paths emerge where dreams reside.

And though the winds may strike anew,
Our roots run deep, our aim is true.
In the wake of storms, we rise,
With hope forever in our eyes.

An Indomitable Presence

In shadows cast by twilight's gleam,
There stands a force, a distant dream.
Untouched by time, undimmed by fear,
An indomitable presence here.

Through shifting winds and changing tide,
With silent grace, it does abide.
A beacon strong, a guiding flame,
In whispered lore, it takes no name.

From ancient roots to unknown skies,
It watches worlds with patient eyes.
An ever-constant guardian's gaze,
Through darkest nights and sunlit days.

Wherever whispers of doubt reside,
Its spirit stands, a force of pride.
An indomitable will, so pure,
A presence timeless, ever sure.

Etched in Bark

Upon the ancient oak they carve,
Tales of old in twisted veins,
Each groove and nook a yearning scar,
Bearing witness to joys and pains.

Seasons brush with gentle hands,
Traces left by passing time,
In the dark, the stories stand,
Whispering in silent rhyme.

Beneath the crescent moon's embrace,
Illuminated softly there,
Love and loss, they interlace,
Leaf and limb, a solemn prayer.

Winter's chill and summer's spark,
Weathered well through countless days,
The memories etched in bark,
Eternal in their quiet ways.

Crown of the Canopy

High above the forest floor,
Where sunlight dances through the leaves,
A kingdom thrives in perfect lore,
Crafted from the whispers of the breeze.

Branches twist in regal grace,
Crowned with verdant waves of green,
Here the trees embrace their space,
In a realm both wild and serene.

Songs of birds fill the air,
In this canopy of life,
Every creature finds its share,
In a world without strife.

From the roots to skyward heights,
Nature reigns in quiet might,
Crown of the canopy, pure delight,
A testament to nature's light.

Endurance in Silence

In woods where shadows softly creep,
Stands a fortress built with pride,
Through the nights, it holds its peace,
Whispering not a single sigh.

Winds may rage and storms may moan,
Yet steadfast in its silent place,
Eons pass, it stands alone,
Endurance etched on its face.

Roots dig deep, unseen below,
With strength drawn from the secret earth,
In silence, it begins to grow,
Life reformed in quiet birth.

When dawn breaks with golden light,
And dusk draws the day to end,
This monument to time's might,
In silence, it continues to mend.

Heart of Timber

Pulled from the heart of forest grand,
Timber stands with stories deep,
Crafted by a careful hand,
Into shapes where secrets sleep.

Furniture to cradle dreams,
Homes where laughter softly blooms,
Through each age with gentle beams,
Bearing lives in silent rooms.

Ships that sail the endless blue,
Harbored by their wooden grace,
In their holds, adventures true,
Lovingly in planks embraced.

Timber heart in each pure grain,
Strength and warmth their essence keep,
Lives entwined in joy and strain,
In the heart of timber, secrets sleep.

Beneath Evergreen Skies

Under an emerald canopy,
Whispers of ancient trees,
A world where shadows play,
And time drifts with the breeze.

Sunlight filters golden,
Through boughs of tranquil green,
Creating a living mosaic,
A forest's serene sheen.

Birdsong floats like whispers,
Secrets told to leaves,
An orchestra of nature,
A promise that never leaves.

Footsteps tread but lightly,
On paths that nature lays,
Each step a quiet reverence,
For woodland's sacred ways.

Here, peace is perennial,
A temple of the wild,
Where life breathes with harmony,
And man returns to child.

Keeper of Forest Secrets

Deep within the ancient wood,
Where sunlight's grip is meek,
Lives the keeper of the secrets,
Of which no man may speak.

Silent as a shadow moves,
Through realms of green and gold,
Guarding whispers of the leaves,
And tales the wind has told.

Eyes like amber, ears like shells,
Attuned to nature's song,
A sentinel of ages past,
Where spirits still belong.

In the hush of twilight's breath,
When stars begin to gleam,
The keeper walks the forest paths,
Protecting every dream.

Ever watchful, ever wise,
In nature's grand embrace,
The keeper holds the forest's heart,
In a timeless, sacred place.

Weathering the Storm

In the heart of thunder's roar,
Where the sky and earth collide,
There lies the strength to endure,
And courage to abide.

Winds may howl with fury,
As lightning splits the night,
But roots dig deep, unwavering,
Through nature's fiercest might.

The trees may bend, but never break,
As rain cascades in streams,
They weather every tempest's rage,
Protecting silent dreams.

When clouds disperse, the calm unfolds,
A world reborn anew,
The storm, a distant memory,
The sky, a brighter blue.

In nature's trial, lessons learned,
Of resilience and grace,
For every storm that we endure,
A stronger, heartier place.

Roots Deep and Untangle

Beneath the earth, a network grows,
Of roots that twist and weave,
Connecting life in silent strength,
In ways you can't conceive.

They delve into the rich, dark soil,
A hidden world beneath,
Anchoring tall and ancient trees,
To secrets they bequeath.

With every branch that sways above,
A story's intertwined,
Of roots that spread like whispered thoughts,
In nature's grand design.

Untangled paths, a labyrinth,
Of life that's intertwined,
In unseen bonds that hold the earth,
To whispers of the mind.

So let us tread with reverence,
On ground where roots run deep,
For in their hidden, tangled strength,
Nature's wisdom we keep.

Guardian of the Forest

Beneath the ancient canopy,
Where whispers never cease,
A figure stands in shadows cast,
Its presence pledging peace.

With eyes that mirror twilight skies,
And heartbeats sync with earth,
This guardian of the thwarted path,
Gives every creature worth.

Leaves rustle soft in gentle breeze,
A lullaby for dusk,
While moonlight dances on the leaves,
With silver's tender husk.

Through night and day, it watches close,
This steward's noble quest,
In emerald boughs, 'neath heaven's glow,
It finds eternal rest.

Seasons of Perseverance

Spring's gentle kiss on tender buds,
Awakes the dormant dreams,
A symphony of life begins,
In soft and vibrant streams.

Summer's sun with fervent fire,
Ignites the will to strive,
In golden fields and azure skies,
Our deepest hopes revive.

Autumn whispers tales of change,
With leaves in rustling dance,
Through fading light and colors bright,
New chances to advance.

Winter's chill may test our strength,
With snow-capped, silent ground,
Yet in the heart, a flame burns on,
With perseverance crowned.

Echoes of Ageless Wisdom

In hallways vast of ancient stone,
Where echoes softly tread,
The voices of the days long gone,
Speak truths we've often read.

With ink from stars and parchment night,
Their wisdom weaves a tale,
Of dreams once born in moonlight's eye,
And hearts that hope prevails.

Each whisper guides with gentle hand,
Through shadows long and deep,
Bestows the courage to withstand,
The secrets time does keep.

Eternal lessons, ageless words,
Reside in walls so grand,
Echoes of the wise endure,
To lead through wisdom's hand.

An Unyielding Sentinel

Amid the storms and thundering skies,
A lone and mighty tree,
Stands firm against the tempest's rage,
An endless canopy.

With roots dug deep in earthen heart,
And branches spread so wide,
It shelters all beneath its boughs,
Through ebb and flow of tide.

Its leaves may fall, its bark may wear,
Yet ever does it stand,
A symbol of resilience pure,
In nature's sprawling land.

An unyielding sentinel in green,
Through seasons' ever flow,
Reminds us of the strength within,
No matter winds that blow.

Through Storms It Stands

Against the wind's fierce howl,
It bends but does not break.
In thunder's ruthless prowl,
Its roots an anchor make.

The rain may drench its leaves,
And lightning etches scars.
Yet still, each dawn it weaves,
Resilience by the stars.

For through the tempest's rage,
Its spirit's steady course.
In nature's endless stage,
It finds a silent force.

Through storms, its strength refined,
A testament so grand.
In nature's heart, aligned,
Through storms, it firmly stands.

Roots of Tenacity

Beneath the soil it's strong,
A network underground.
In silence, it belongs,
No mightier can be found.

The roots stretch far and wide,
In search of life's sweet streams.
Their journey magnified,
In nature's quiet dreams.

Each tendril, each embrace,
A testament to grit.
In life's unending race,
It's never one to quit.

Through seasons harsh and mild,
Its courage never fades.
In earth's purest compiled,
Where tenacity pervades.

Legacy of Green Giants

In forests deep, they rise,
These titans of the green.
Their branches touch the skies,
A sight so rarely seen.

Majestic in their height,
Each year they upward grow.
Through day and darkest night,
Their wisdom seems to show.

They've witnessed endless tales,
Of ages come and gone.
Their leaves whispering trails,
Of eras passed at dawn.

These giants tell their lore,
In silence, tall and grand.
Our footprints, evermore,
Upon their legacy, stand.

Beneath the Timeless Canopy

A shelter from the sun,
In boughs so wide and vast.
When daylight's course is run,
Its shadows long will last.

The whispers in the leaves,
Of secrets old and new.
The heart that so believes,
In magic all but true.

A dome of emerald green,
A ceiling of pure grace.
Below, a tranquil scene,
A truly sacred space.

Through years of endless time,
It guards both old and young.
Beneath this canopy, prime,
Nature's song is sung.

Winter's Bare Embrace

Snowflakes dance in silent grace,
Gentle whispers, nature's lace.
Naked trees in still repose,
Adorned in winter's quiet clothes.

Footsteps crunch on icy ground,
Echoes lost, without a sound.
Breath hangs heavy, visibly,
In winter's hold, steadfastly.

Grey skies loom above the land,
Frigid touch on numbing hand.
Frost-etched windows, crystal clear,
Whisper tales for us to hear.

Fireside warmth, sweet retreat,
From the world's cold, bitter beat.
Shadows flicker on the walls,
As winter's chill outside calls.

Silent night in starlit glow,
Blanket white of purest snow.
In this still and frozen place,
Lies winter's bare embrace.

Spring's New Breath

Buds unfold with morning light,
Birdsong weaves the air so bright.
Emerald fields and blooming trees,
Spring’s renewal on the breeze.

Soft rains fall on thirsty earth,
Whisper promises of birth.
Daffodils and tulips rise,
Greet the sun with joyful eyes.

Warmth awakens, life is stirred,
Nature’s symphony is heard.
Butterflies in painted dress,
Dance amid the wilderness.

Days grow longer, nights grow mild,
Springtime’s spirit, fresh and wild.
Paths once hidden now in view,
Spring’s embrace, a world anew.

Hope reclaims the winter's blight,
Colors burst in sheer delight.
Every breath and every sight,
Sings of spring's new breath tonight.

Summer's Green Crown

Fields of green beneath the sun,
Beckon all to join the fun.
Golden rays and skies of blue,
Summer’s kiss, a dream anew.

Whispers of the rustling leaves,
Glimmering through the balmy eves.
Soft caress of warm night air,
Perfumed gardens, blooms so fair.

Ocean waves in steady beat,
Cool relief from earth’s fierce heat.
Children's laughter, boundless cheer,
Echoes through the atmosphere.

Fireflies light twilight’s shroud,
Nature’s lanterns, small yet proud.
Moonlit paths of shadowed grace,
Guide the wand’rer to their place.

Harvest moons and endless days,
Painted in the sun’s warm rays.
This green crown, so proudly worn,
Heralds summer’s golden morn.

Windswept and Unbroken

Whispers ride on zephyrs fair,
Through the meadow, everywhere.
Bending grasses, wild and free,
All unite in harmony.

Mountains kiss the clear blue sky,
Standing firm, they testify.
Winds may howl with strength untamed,
Yet their cores remain unclaimed.

Leaves dance to the tempest's song,
Weaving patterns, weak and strong.
Nature's breath in ebb and flow,
Tales of life in gusts bestow.

Oceans churn with mighty force,
Waves that crash without remorse.
Yet with every tempest's rage,
Comes the calm, the turning page.

Hearts unbroken in the gale,
Find their strength when others fail.
Through the storm, they steadfast stand,
Windswept souls as grains of sand.

Pillars of the Earth

Beneath an endless sky of blue,
Where ancient roots run deep and true,
Stand pillars proud, unyielding stone,
Guardians of the lands unknown.

Their shadows stretch across the years,
Echoing past a thousand tears,
Through storm and sun, they've held their place,
Timeless silence on nature's face.

Mountains high and valleys low,
Echo stories of long ago,
Whispered secrets in the wind,
Of where the earth and heaven blend.

Carved by forces fierce yet grand,
They shape the contours of the land,
Silent strength in rock and clay,
Guiding us upon our way.

Beacons through the mists of time,
Monuments to the earth's design,
Steadfast sentinels they remain,
Pillars of the earth's refrain.

Seasons in Stillness

In winter's hush, the world holds still,
Frozen lakes and frosted hill,
Silent breath of the cold night air,
Crystals twinkling everywhere.

Springtime stirs with gentle breeze,
Emerald buds on naked trees,
Softly whispers life anew,
Nature's promise, bold and true.

Summer's warmth with golden light,
Days stretch long from morn to night,
In fields of green, the flowers bloom,
Filling hearts with rich perfume.

Autumn brings a fiery kiss,
Crimson leaves in swirling bliss,
Fallen beauty paints the ground,
Nature's symphony in sound.

Each season in its quiet way,
Marks the passage of the day,
In stillness, we find the rhyme,
Woven into the threads of time.

From Acorn to Titan

From humble acorn, mighty tree,
Roots entwined with destiny,
Through seasons' trials, steadfast grows,
Strength born deep where no one knows.

Tiny seedling, fragile start,
With iron bark, and iron heart,
Faces storms and stands its ground,
In its branches, life is found.

Years pass on, the tree expands,
Reaching out with aged hands,
Casting shadows, wide and great,
Testament to nature's fate.

From forest floor to lofty skies,
Titans rise before our eyes,
Branches creak with ancient song,
Holding memories all along.

As time rolls on, the cycle spins,
Mighty trees will shed their skin,
But from acorn, small and bright,
Grows the titan, towering height.

Echoes in the Timberland

Amidst the forest, shadows play,
Where light and dark do gently sway,
Timber whispers, ancient sound,
Echoes in the wood resound.

Through winding paths and hidden nooks,
Nature writes its secret books,
Leaves are pages, trees are tomes,
Silent stories far from homes.

Birds call out in vibrant cheer,
In timberland, they sing so clear,
Melodies that drift away,
Echoes meant to guide our way.

Deep within the forest floor,
Whispers voices of folklore,
Legends old, a truth they weave,
In the bough and in the leaf.

Walk through timberland with grace,
Feel the echoes, find your place,
Nature's pulse will lead you on,
Until the final echo's gone.

Old Roots, New Leaves

In the soil where dreams take hold,
A story ancient, oft retold,
Roots dig deep, unseen, and bold,
From hidden strength, new leaves unfold.

Seasons change, as whispers weave,
Time's embrace, in what we believe,
Through storm and sunlight they achieve,
Their dance of life, they n'er deceive.

Generations stand in awe,
Witnessing what nature saw,
From softest silk to sturdy straw,
Each leaf a testament to law.

Roots that anchor, leaves that sway,
Together in the light of day,
Bound by earth from which they stray,
Old and new in perfect play.

Hope and history intertwine,
A lineage of the divine,
Forever flowing, line by line,
In roots below and leaves that shine.

Unyielding Bark

Beneath the sky, through seasons wild,
A tree stands tall, untamed, and mild,
In weather's ire, serene and styled,
Its bark is unyielding, wisdom piled.

Each scar it bears, a silent tale,
Of winds that howled, and storms that wail,
Yet never does its courage fail,
In steadfast strength, it will prevail.

The sun may scorch, the winters freeze,
It bends not to the harshest breeze,
A guardian 'midst the forest seas,
Its bark a fortress, roots with ease.

Time may pass, and leaves may fall,
Yet still it stands, above them all,
In quiet grace, and actions tall,
Its essence spreads, a timeless call.

From age to age, unchanging still,
A bastion strong upon the hill,
In nature's heart, it finds its thrill,
An unyielding bark, through force and will.

Guardians of the Grove

Within the grove where whispers sing,
The guardians stand, a sacred ring,
Their branches stretch, a living wing,
In shade, the forest's heart they bring.

In quiet watch, they hold their ground,
Their roots enmeshed, so deeply wound,
Between the trees, no space is found,
In unity, their love is bound.

Through morning's mist and twilight's haze,
They stand as sentinels, unfazed,
In sunlit glows or shadowed maze,
Their vigil constant, always raised.

The wildlife seeks their haven near,
A sylvan realm where hearts may clear,
A whisper soft, a call sincere,
The guardians hold what we hold dear.

Their timeless watch, a pledge unbroke,
In leaves and wood and sapling's cloak,
In grove's embrace, they softly spoke,
Of life and promise, tree and oak.

Forest's Heartbeat

In the quiet depths where shadows creep,
There lies a rhythm, strong and deep,
A heartbeat of the forest, steep,
In secrets that the ancients keep.

The whisper of the leaves at night,
The murmurs soft in dawn's first light,
A symphony that takes its flight,
In boughs and branches, taking height.

Life pulses through each verdant vein,
In drops of dew, in fall of rain,
In summer's glow, in winter's strain,
The heartbeat thunders, yet remains.

With every breath the forest sighs,
A song of life beneath the skies,
In emerald hues, it never lies,
Its rhythm true, through lows and highs.

In every step, in every beat,
The woodland's pulse, serene, discreet,
A cycle endless, pure and sweet,
The forest's heartbeat, strong and complete.

Lifetime of Shadows

In twilight's gentle embrace,
Whispers of days gone by,
A shadow's tender trace,
Against the evening sky.

Memories softly fall,
Like leaves from ancient trees,
Silent echoes call,
Swirling in the breeze.

Years stitched in twilight's hues,
Night's quiet serenade,
Half-forgotten views,
Where light begins to fade.

Dreams waltz in moonlit halls,
Specters of time's embrace,
In the timeless thrall,
Of shadows' tender grace.

Beneath the starry veil,
In shadows we reside,
A lifetime's whispered tale,
In shadows we confide.

Standing Tall and True

In forests wild and free,
Amidst the verdant green,
Stands a tree mighty,
With a crown serene.

Against storms and sunlit days,
Branches reach the sky,
In steadfast, ancient ways,
Its spirit flying high.

Roots deep in the earth,
Holding stories old,
Eternal in its worth,
A tale of strength untold.

Under a canopy wide,
Life's whispers softly flow,
With dignity and pride,
In the winds that blow.

From seed to mighty oak,
Time's endless dance ensues,
A testament bespoke,
Standing tall and true.

Trees of Fortitude

Centuries entwined,
In silence and in grace,
Through every age defined,
By time's unyielding pace.

Beneath the emerald sheen,
Lives wisdom old and bright,
In every leaf that's seen,
A beacon in the night.

Guardians of the land,
With roots like veins of gold,
A testament so grand,
To stories never told.

Each branch whispers tales,
Of epochs long since passed,
In gentle, rustling veils,
Their legacy is cast.

Steadfast they endure,
In sun and rain and snow,
Fortitude so pure,
In their eternal glow.

Autumn's Golden Armor

A dance of fiery hues,
Upon the autumn breeze,
Leaves in varied cues,
Murmur through the trees.

Golden armor spread,
Across the woodland wide,
Nature's softest bed,
Where scarlet secrets hide.

In twilight's amber glow,
Mountains of rust unfold,
As shadows softly grow,
Beneath the burnished gold.

Whispers of the fall,
In every rustling leaf,
A season's gentle call,
In moments oh so brief.

With nature's grand display,
Before the winter's chill,
In golden, grand array,
Autumn's magic thrills.

Strength in the Storm

Beneath the darkened, swirling skies,
Resilient hearts rise, shining bright,
Through gusts that rage and torrents cry,
They find their strength in stormy night.

Each drop that falls is fuel anew,
For spirits anchored, steady, sure,
With every thunder, courage grew,
To face the tempest and endure.

Amid the chaos, voices blend,
A symphony of hope and fight,
For every stormy gale they fend,
They stand together in the light.

Unyielding will, their silent song,
Resilience etched in every vein,
Through every storm they march along,
A testament to strength in pain.

When calm returns and skies are clear,
They'll rest, but never truly tire,
For in their hearts, the storm is near,
And strength remains, an eternal fire.

Roots of Endurance

Deep within the soil's embrace,
Lies the steadfast, silent force,
Roots that weave through time and space,
Holding strong their ancient course.

Buried where the shadows creep,
Far from sunlight's tender cheer,
They whisper stories, secrets deep,
Of endurance through each year.

Against the pulling tides of time,
These roots endure, steadfast and stout,
In silence they perform their climb,
Their journey never filled with doubt.

Though storms above may fiercely sway,
And tempests surge against their ground,
These roots remain, their strength display,
In steadfast silence, they're unbound.

From roots of endurance, greatness springs,
A testament to patience long,
Through countless winters, endless springs,
Roots sing their unyielding songs.

Whispers of the Ancient Tree

Underneath the moon's soft glow,
Ancient branches creak and sigh,
Whispers from the long ago,
Stories told beneath the sky.

Leaves that rustle, secrets share,
Wind that carries tales once spun,
Mysteries linger in the air,
Of days beneath a younger sun.

From the roots to high above,
Time has etched its patterned art,
Whispers of the tree, thereof,
Speak to every beating heart.

Through the ages, standing tall,
Witness to both joy and pain,
The ancient tree has seen it all,
Whispering truths in wind and rain.

Beneath its boughs, the world unfolds,
Echoes of a time set free,
Within its bark, the past it holds,
Whispers of eternity.

Standing Tall Through Time

Amid the shifting sands of fate,
Stands a figure, bold and true,
Time's relentless, patient gait,
Could never sway, nor bid adieu.

Through seasons' dance and shadows' play,
Firmly rooted, resolute,
Years may come and swiftly sway,
Yet this spirit won't dilute.

Mountains high and valleys low,
Witness to a steadfast heart,
Through the ages' ebb and flow,
Standing tall, an artful part.

Against the tide of fleeting years,
Unyielding, solid, strong remains,
A guardian through joys and tears,
Resilience flowing through its veins.

In the tapestry of time,
Weaving strength in every thread,
Standing tall in every climb,
Through centuries, this truth is spread.

Elders of the Woodland

Beneath the ancient canopy, they stand,
Silent guardians of the fertile land.
Roots entwined in stories, old and grand,
Their leaves whisper secrets, so unplanned.

Time passes gently, in their serene reign,
Seasons merge, yet they remain.
Whispers of wisdom in each vein,
Holding the forest's answers, plain.

Majestic figures, cloaked in green,
Witnesses to what has been.
Their knowledge vast, but unseen,
Nature's wisdom, pure and keen.

From acorns to towering oak,
They've seen the seed of life provoke.
Through storms and droughts, they spoke,
Resilience, in each timeless stroke.

Elders of this sacred place,
Holding time in their embrace.
In their presence, find your space,
Feel the forest's gentle grace.

Beneath the Leafy Fortress

Underneath the foliage, shadows play,
A fortress green where spirits stay.
In peaceful silence, night and day,
Life’s gentle hum holds sway.

Twilight dances through the leaves,
Whispering tales the mind receives.
Where the heart in quiet believes,
In magic spun by nature’s weaves.

A sanctuary of life, profound,
With roots that twist beneath the ground.
Where whispers of the past are found,
In echoes soft, without a sound.

Within this shelter, creatures roam,
Finding solace, calling it home.
In this leafy, sacred dome,
In unity, the forest's poem.

Stand beneath and feel its might,
A leafy fortress, pure delight.
In its heart, both day and night,
Find peace within the nature's sight.

Longevity in Leaves

In the greenest leaves, life’s tale is spun,
From dawn's first light to setting sun.
In every leaf, a battle won,
Against the forces that would shun.

Year by year, they cling with grace,
Marking time, each in its place.
In their veins, life’s silent race,
Endurance found, a warm embrace.

Seasons change, yet still they stand,
Nature’s map, by time’s hand planned.
Holding secrets, oh so grand,
Longevity, where leaves expand.

Colors shift from green to gold,
Stories in the wind are told.
In each leaf, a truth to hold,
The essence of the seasons' fold.

From the bud of a tender spring,
To autumn's end, when branches sing.
Longevity in leaves shall bring,
Life's full circle, an endless ring.

Songs of the Silent Forest

Beneath the canopy, a gentle tune,
Echoes in the light of the moon.
Songs of pines, in rhythmic swoon,
Nature’s quiet, morning to noon.

Birds and breeze compose the score,
In harmony, forevermore.
Within the silence, hear the lore,
The forest's heart, its ancient core.

Whispers of the leaves in air,
Songs of peace, everywhere.
In the silence, a world so rare,
Melodies of nature’s care.

From dawning light to dusky hue,
The forest sings, old and new.
Voices pure, and through and through,
In each note, a story grew.

Silent forest, harmonious blend,
Songs that time cannot transcend.
In their beauty, find a friend,
Musical tales that never end.

Echoes Through the Canopy

Hushed whispers weave a tale,
Among the leaves, they sail,
Soft murmurs of the breeze,
Through ancient, whispering trees.

A canopy of jade,
Where light and shadow wade,
Nature's lullaby hums,
To the beat of silent drums.

Footsteps of the past,
In shadowed groves, they cast,
Echoes of life once bright,
Now caught in nature’s night.

Beneath the emerald shroud,
The forest stands so proud,
A symphony of green,
In a dance of the unseen.

The old trees guard the tale,
Where time and life prevail,
In twilight’s gentle hold,
Their secrets softly told.

Windswept Guardian

Upon the rugged crest,
A sentinel stands at rest,
With branches wide unfurled,
To shelter a weary world.

The wind sings ancient songs,
Through limbs where history throngs,
Each gust a tender sigh,
Of mem'ries drifting by.

Roots deep in ageless earth,
A testament of worth,
Whispers of time's caress,
In nature's quiet dress.

Leaves dance in twilight's glow,
In patterns soft and slow,
Guarding the land with grace,
From their steadfast, sacred place.

In every rustling leaf,
Tales of joy and grief,
The windswept guardian stands,
Holding the world in hands.

Giant of Quiet Resilience

A giant, towering high,
Against the azure sky,
Strength in every vein,
Through sun and storm and rain.

A silent watch it keeps,
While the world around it sleeps,
Unyielding, firm, and true,
In days dark, green, and blue.

Rings of eternal time,
Mark its silent climb,
A record of the years,
Of joy, of sweat, of tears.

Leaves of emerald hue,
Reflect the morning dew,
In its shade, life finds peace,
A moment's sweet release.

Stalwart and ever wise,
With roots where ancient secrets lie,
The giant stands, serene,
A steadfast forest dream.

The Old One's Vigil

Under a moonlit sky,
The old one stands so high,
Guarding through the night,
With a heart of purest light.

Through seasons' endless flow,
In sun and winter’s snow,
Its watch is never done,
From dawn to setting sun.

Shadows dance and fade,
Beneath its boughs of jade,
A silent, steadfast seer,
Of time and tide so near.

Cradled in the breeze,
Its story told in leaves,
A vigil pure and bright,
In the calm and quiet night.

Life's whispers it has known,
Through ages, it has grown,
The old one’s timeless sight,
A beacon in the night.

Roots Deep and Strong

In the quiet ground, roots intertwine,
Life pulses deep beneath unseen line.
Silent whispers to the trees belong,
Guardians of earth, roots deep and strong.

Nourished by soil, the lifeblood flows,
Every branch above in union grows.
Sturdy in storms, they face the throng,
Firm and steadfast, roots deep and strong.

Through seasons' change, unwavering stay,
Binding the land in their steadfast way.
Below the surface, an ancient song,
Melody of life, roots deep and strong.

Standing in Silent Grace

Beneath the sky, in tranquil place,
Majestic presence, silent grace.
Witness to time's unhurried pace,
They stand, enduring, in their space.

Leaves whisper secrets to the wind,
Stories of old, where life begins.
Shadows dance, their silent face,
Marked by nature's gentle trace.

Quiet strength in every stance,
In moonlit glow or daylight's dance.
Eternally poised, with endless chase,
Standing tall in silent grace.

Echoes of Survival

From the depths of time, resilience found,
Echoes of histories in silent sound.
Survival etched on rugged ground,
In every leaf and trunk, profound.

Scars of fire, weather's wear,
Testaments to the strength they bear.
Unbowed by fate's relentless trial,
Whispered tales of survival.

Cycles of time in every ring,
A symphony of enduring things.
Life persists, despite denial,
In their roots, echoes of survival.

Keeper of Ancient Secrets

In aged bark, the stories dwell,
Ancient secrets, none can tell.
Guardians of a time-worn spell,
In silent forests, they prevail.

Witness to the earth's old ways,
Silent keepers of forgotten days.
Under canopies where shadows play,
Histories hidden in their sway.

Each branch a tome, each leaf a page,
Chronicles of an ancient age.
In their presence, wisdom seeps,
Keeper of secrets, the forest keeps.

Story of the Stout Tree

In a meadow vast, a tree once stood,
With roots deep in the ancient wood,
Its branches wide, a shelter found,
A tale of life, on sacred ground.

Through seasons harsh, winds wild and free,
This stalwart tree stood stout and free,
With leaves that whispered secrets old,
An ageless story, brave and bold.

Through rain and storm, it did not sway,
A guardian of both night and day,
Its bark a testament to time,
A living poem, nature's rhyme.

It sheltered birds, and gave them flight,
Through darkest night and morning light,
A symbol of enduring grace,
A steadfast friend, in nature's space.

Now as the suns set, endlessly,
The spirit lives, within the tree,
In hearts of those who pass it by,
A legend reaching to the sky.

Timeless Refuge

Beneath the arch of skies so blue,
A refuge waits for me and you,
Its walls of time, both strong and kind,
A haven soothing heart and mind.

It whispers tales of ages past,
A sanctuary built to last,
With every stone, a story known,
A place where weary souls have grown.

Amid the songs of rustling leaves,
Eternal shadows, tangled eves,
This timeless refuge, calm, serene,
A dream of days and nights unseen.

Through endless paths of winding streams,
It guards the hopes, the twirling dreams,
With whispers soft and breezes light,
A beacon in the darkest night.

So let us find this sacred space,
Where time and peace in silence race,
A refuge held within our hearts,
A timeless gift, as life departs.

Through Countless Summers

The summer sun, it brightly gleams,
On fields ablaze with golden dreams,
Each ray a brush on canvas wide,
A tapestry where hope can hide.

Through countless summers, days unfold,
In hues of amber, red, and gold,
With laughter echoing through days,
And nightfall draped in twilight's haze.

The scent of blooms, a fragrant sigh,
In warm embrace, the earth and sky,
Each moment casts a magic spell,
A story only time can tell.

With every dawn, a promise new,
In colors bold, in skies of blue,
Through countless summers, joys renew,
The heart recalls, as love ensues.

As seasons pass and summers wane,
Their memories, in hearts remain,
A symphony of sunlit dreams,
Through endless summers' glowing beams.

Majesty in Adversity

When storm clouds gather, fierce and wild,
And nature's wrath runs unbeguiled,
A strength within begins to rise,
A force unseen by mortal eyes.

In valleys deep and mountains high,
Through trials that make the spirit sigh,
There blooms a majesty so grand,
In every heart, in every land.

For in the face of dire dismay,
A courage grows, it lights the way,
With every challenge, fierce and stark,
A brighter spark ignites the dark.

The soul finds wings where none were near,
A testament to quell all fear,
In times of strife, with heads held high,
A majesty that nears the sky.

For strength is born of stormy seas,
In moments fraught with fear’s unease,
A majesty in adversity,
A force of love, of liberty.

Forest's Silent Warrior

In shadows deep, where light is sparse,
A giant stands with steadfast heart.
Its roots dig deep, its limbs reach high,
Silent guardian of the sky.

Through wind and storm, it sways yet stays,
A sentinel through night and days.
Leaves whisper tales of ancient lore,
Of times and trials it saw before.

Emerald cloak and bark of might,
It braves the whispers of the night.
With each dawn's light, it breathes anew,
A saga of the earth it grew.

Amidst the hush of twilight's breath,
It shields the forest from unseen death.
A colossus of the wooded land,
Protector of nature's gentle hand.

In twilight’s glow, in dawning's gleam,
Its strength and grace forever beam.
A steadfast force, a timeless stay,
The forest's silent warrior, day by day.

Unbowed by Time

In ancient groves where spirits flow,
There stands a live oak, old and slow.
With limbs that tell of centuries past,
Each ring within, a time held fast.

Weathered skin and gnarled form,
It braves the fiercest southern storm.
Through drought and flood, it digs in deep,
Holding memories, roots that keep.

A haven for the wandering bird,
Its leaves have heard what hearts have stirred.
From lovers' vows to solemn cries,
It guards the secrets of the skies.

Beneath its arch, the shadows play,
In whispers soft, the winds convey.
An echo of the ages gone,
A sentinel from dusk to dawn.

Unbowed by time’s unyielding touch,
It stands, revered, a silent hush.
Majestic, bold, against the strife,
A testament to enduring life.

Heritage of Strength

In fields where battles once were fought,
A towering oak, with wisdom sought.
Its scars are tales of valor told,
Of warriors brave and hearts of gold.

With branches wide, it touches sky,
A living link to days gone by.
Its leaves are whispers on the breeze,
A legacy among the trees.

Through wars and peace, it firmly stands,
A beacon in these hallowed lands.
Its roots entwine with blood and soil,
A testament to endless toil.

Children play 'neath shade it casts,
Unaware of trials past.
Its strength is silent, yet it speaks,
Of courage found in those who seek.

Majestic in the morning light,
It stands, a symbol of the fight.
With grace and power intertwined,
A heritage of strength defined.

Seasons of Standing Firm

In springtime’s bloom, when life renews,
The oak stands tall amidst the hues.
Young leaves unfold in morning’s light,
A promise of the coming night.

Through summer’s blaze, with heat intense,
Its leaves provide a cool defense.
A shield from sun, a verdant dome,
A refuge known to all as home.

In autumn’s glow, with colors bright,
Its majesty is pure delight.
Golden leaves descend like rain,
A cycle of rebirth and gain.

Winter comes with biting cold,
The oak stands firm, its story told.
Bare branches scrape the greyish sky,
Yet life within refuses to die.

Through every season’s ebb and flow,
The oak persists, to stand and grow.
A testament to nature’s will,
Standing firm and steadfast still.

A Saga of Strength

In lands where shadows deeply spread,
The warriors rise with hearts like lead,
Their courage crafted, spirits blend,
A saga of strength that has no end.

Through battles fierce and nights so long,
They march with valor, bold and strong,
The echoes of their fight is song,
A saga of strength where they belong.

In every wound, a tale they weave,
With every scar, a truth they leave,
In unity, they do believe,
A saga of strength, they won't deceive.

With swords of hope and shields of pride,
Against the storm, they won’t subside,
In brotherhood, they will confide,
A saga of strength walks side by side.

When dawn breaks forth with golden hue,
Their stories told by morning dew,
To battles past, they bid adieu,
A saga of strength, forever true.

Veins of Tenacity

Beneath the crust of trial and tear,
Flows lifeblood fierce, beyond compare,
In rocky paths, through despair,
Veins of tenacity declare.

In hearts unyielding, firm and bright,
Through darkest days and quiet night,
The will to strive, to reach the height,
Veins of tenacity ignite.

With every step, the ground they claim,
Undaunted by the fiercest flame,
Resilience marks their earthly name,
Veins of tenacity proclaim.

In symphony of sweat and dust,
The hands that toil, the souls that trust,
Unfailing bond of steel and rust,
Veins of tenacity adjust.

Thus forward march, with purpose keen,
In every trial, they are seen,
A testament to worlds between,
Veins of tenacity serene.

Whispers Among Ancient Branches

In forest deep with shadows cast,
Ancient branches frame the past,
Their whispers tell of times amassed,
Where secrets in their leaves are clasped.

Through seasons' turns and weather's hand,
They stand as witness, grand and planned,
Their stories spread throughout the land,
In whispers that few understand.

The rustling leaves, a soft refrain,
Of joy and sorrow, love and pain,
In whispers that the winds sustain,
Among the branches they remain.

With every breeze, they intertwine,
The tales of old, the days divine,
In whispers soft, like ancient wine,
The branches whisper, line by line.

So listen close as night descends,
To whispers true, where twilight bends,
In ancient branches, time transcends,
With stories that forever mend.

Echoes of Sturdy Trunks

In grove where giants pierce the sky,
The sturdy trunks stand firm and high,
Their echoes ring as ages fly,
In whispered winds, their secrets lie.

Through countless years they bear their weight,
In steadfast form, defying fate,
Their roots in soil, their stance innate,
Echoes of trunks that resonate.

With every ring, a story told,
Of winters harsh and summers bold,
In echoes from the days of old,
Their presence, timeless, to behold.

The trunks, they speak of courage pure,
Of strength and grace that must endure,
Their whispers clear, their heartbeats sure,
Echoes of trunks that reassure.

So let your heart attune and hear,
The echoes from the trunks so near,
In their embrace, you'll find no fear,
Echoes of trunks, forever dear.

Heart of the Woodland

Deep in the shaded grove, the whispers sing,
Where ancient oaks their noble branches fling,
The heart of the woodland beats, so pure,
A sanctuary, in nature's beauty secure.

Soft moss carpets paths of emerald green,
Sunlight dapples through leaves, creating a sheen,
A chorus of birds in harmonious flight,
Echoing through twilight and dawn's first light.

Amidst the flora, life flourishes unseen,
Foxes tread softly, moving between,
The tranquil hum of life thrives here,
In the heart of the woodland, all is clear.

Seasons pass in a dance of grace,
Autumn leaves fall, winter’s silent embrace,
Spring’s rebirth and summer’s warm glow,
All cycle through, in nature’s endless flow.

May this woodland heart forever pulsate,
Guarded by time’s relentless gait,
In every rustling leaf and fleeting glance,
The woodland's soul, in eternal dance.

Mighty in Stillness

In the silent vastness, strength is found,
Where echoes of time make not a sound,
Mighty in stillness, the mountains stand,
Guardians of earth, both vast and grand.

Snow crowns their peaks with wintry pride,
Rivers carve valleys by mountainside,
Whispers of ages etched in stone,
Legends of old in each crag known.

Beneath their shadows, life persists,
In silent strength, the world exists,
From dawn's first light to twilight's gleam,
The silent grandeur, a timeless dream.

Clouds gently kiss their ancient face,
In their presence, chaos finds its place,
A steadfast watch through night and day,
In the stillness, might finds its way.

May we draw from their endless peace,
The strength to endure, to never cease,
Standing firm against life's tempestuous tide,
Mighty in stillness, with dignity and pride.

Unbroken by the Wind

Against the tempest, resilient they stand,
Trees unyielding in a storm-swept land,
Their roots dig deep, their branches wide,
Unbroken by the wind, with nature they abide.

Each gust a challenge, each storm a test,
Yet they remain, unchanging, at rest,
Leaves may fall, and trunks may bend,
But their spirits, nature's force can mend.

Through howling nights and shadowed skies,
They whisper truths and ancient sighs,
A testament to endurance and grace,
Embracing each element, each fierce embrace.

Seasons bring change, time moves on,
Yet through it all, they remain strong,
In every leaf, a story is spun,
Of battles fought, of victories won.

Unbroken by the wind, they inspire,
A symbol of life's unyielding fire,
May we too stand, steadfast and kind,
Rooted in resilience, with a mighty mind.

Timeless Fortitude

Beneath azure skies, under twilight's hue,
Mountains endure, ancient and true,
Timeless fortitude carved in stone,
Whispers of ages, in wind, are blown.

Centuries pass, they witness it all,
From dawn’s birth to night’s call,
Their unyielding peaks reach for the stars,
Bearing the scars of cosmic wars.

In valleys below, life ebbs and flows,
While above, eternal strength glows,
Weathered by time, unbroken they stay,
Monuments to persistence, come what may.

Rivers may carve, and storms may rage,
But they stand firm, through every age,
A beacon of endurance in nature’s vast embrace,
With unshakable resolve, they occupy their space.

May we draw from their endless might,
In our own battles, stand upright,
With timeless fortitude in every deed,
Unyielding in spirit, in thought, in creed.

Nature’s Watchtower

Amidst the tranquil forest deep,
A watchtower stands, its secrets keep.
O'er hills, its gaze forever casts,
Silent sentinel of days long past.

Whispering winds around it play,
In hues of dawn and twilight's ray.
Trees sway gently, a loyal choir,
To nature’s will, their hearts aspire.

Clouds drift lazily in the blue,
Mirroring lakes in crystal hue.
A hawk circles, vigilant and free,
Guarding the realm from sky to tree.

Moonlight cloaks the watchtower’s form,
As stars begin their nightly swarm.
The world beneath in quiet sleep,
Beneath the watchtower's steadfast keep.

Seasons pass, yet it stands tall,
Witness to the earth’s gentle sprawl.
Timeless in its guarded grace,
Nature’s watchtower holds its place.

Gnarled but Not Broken

In the heart of ancient woods so deep,
Where shadows lay and secrets sleep.
A tree stands tall, gnarled and old,
Its stories in its branches told.

Beneath the bark, a spirit fights,
Against the storms and darkest nights.
With roots entrenched in earth’s embrace,
Its strength time never could erase.

Winds howl, yet it does not cower,
Firm in its enduring power.
Leaves may fall with autumn’s kiss,
But winters pass, and spring’s new bliss.

Scars it bears, from years gone by,
Underneath the ever-changing sky.
Yet it remains, unbowed and proud,
A king beneath a leafy shroud.

For in its heart, a lesson lies,
Strength and grace in nature’s guise.
Though twisted by the hands of time,
Gnarled but not broken, it shall climb.

Among the Whispering Pines

In the forest where the pine trees grow,
Whispers travel with the wind's flow.
Silent secrets in needles green,
Among the whispers, sights unseen.

Shadows dance with morning's light,
A symphony of nature's might.
Paths wind through a sea of calm,
With every step, a healing balm.

Birds sing sonnets to the dawn,
As dew adorns the verdant lawn.
Peaceful moments, hearts align,
Among the whispering pines divine.

Evening's glow turns skies to gold,
As stories of the woods unfold.
Stars emerge in twilight's veil,
To hear the forest's ancient tale.

Stillness in the night's embrace,
Tranquility, a gentle grace.
Life and dreams in harmony,
Among the pines, eternally.

Life Through Leaves

Sunlight pierces the canopy bright,
Casting shadows in forest light.
Through leaves, life's colors softly stream,
A painter's brush on nature's dream.

Each leaf a story, etched in green,
A world within, yet so serene.
Whispered breezes sweetly sing,
Of life through veins, in endless ring.

Raindrops fall in rhythmic grace,
Nature's tears on each leaf's face.
Quenching thirst of earth below,
Starting cycles that softly flow.

Birds take flight, their feathers brush,
Against the sky's resplendent hush.
Life below in leaves is seen,
Mirrored in their vibrant sheen.

Seasons change, yet leaves remain,
Witness to the joy and pain.
In every hue, a pulse that's true,
Life through leaves in endless view.

Beneath a Crown of Leaves

In the forest deep and old,
Where stories whispered, often told,
Beneath a crown of leaves so green,
The ancient guardians are seen.

Winds that hum through branches tight,
Play symphonies in the night,
Moonbeams dance in fearless fawn,
Till the tender break of dawn.

Rivers murmur secrets here,
To trees that lend a patient ear,
Roots run deep, in earth’s embrace,
Time’s swift passage leaves no trace.

Nature's choir gives its praise,
In myriad songs through endless days,
Beneath the leaves, life’s woven there,
In fabric fine beyond compare.

Thus, 'neath the crown of leaves we find,
An essence pure, a peace of mind,
In shadows cool and whispers kind,
With nature’s heart, forever twined.

Silent Sovereign

In halls where echoes softly roam,
The Silent Sovereign claims their throne,
With grace and peace they quiet reign,
O'er lands that feel no mortal pain.

Their kingdom vast, horizon wide,
Compassion's glow their only guide,
No speech is needed to command,
For love and kindness rule the land.

Stars above in reverence bow,
To wisdom's light that shows the how,
A silent voice, yet clear and true,
A beacon bright for all to view.

Mountains rise in stately grace,
Their peaks where heavens softly trace,
In silence they their secrets keep,
In peaceful watch, the Sovereign sleeps.

In harmony, the world does turn,
With every heart a lesson learned,
Silent Sovereign, wise and kind,
Leaves paths of light for us to find.

Strength in Stillness

Beneath the sky in colors cast,
A tranquil pond reflects the past,
Strength in stillness calmly lies,
In whispered winds and quiet sighs.

Mountains hold the dawn's embrace,
In silent power, firm in place,
Through quiet strength they stand the test,
Inviting all to pause and rest.

In moments hushed, the heart can heal,
With silent truths that still reveal,
Connections vast, unseen yet real,
In the calm, our spirits feel.

The forest deep, the meadow wide,
In stillness find their souls' abide,
Echoes speak of time's long flow,
In silence, ancient spirits grow.

Find your peace in moments clear,
Where quiet strength speaks free of fear,
With strength in stillness as your guide,
Embrace the calm, let peace reside.

Roots Entwined with Time

In the cradle of the earth,
Where time and life give gentle birth,
Roots entwined with soils deep,
In nature's arms they softly sleep.

Lonely trees that touch the sky,
With branches reaching high and high,
Their roots in silent wisdom hold,
The stories ancient, secrets old.

Seasons come and seasons go,
Yet roots in strength persist and grow,
Bound by years yet free as breeze,
They anchor firm through all degrees.

History’s breath in leaves does sigh,
Through roots that twine and mystify,
Boundaries old, forgotten lines,
In nature’s course, through roots, defines.

Thus, in roots entwined with time,
We find a reason, find the rhyme,
A connection pure, forever tied,
In nature’s arms, where dreams abide.

Woodland Resilience

In verdant groves where shadows play,
Strength is born from night and day,
Roots dig deep and branches rise,
'Neath the ever-changing skies.

Songs of resilience in each leaf,
Whispers of ancient belief,
Through storm and sun they stand tall,
Nature heeds resilience's call.

Silent strength in quiet woods,
Unspoken laws and understood,
Every fallen leaf renews,
Hope in shades of mingling hues.

Seasons change but still they hold,
Secrets in their bark enfold,
Cycles end and then begin,
In the heart where life is kin.

Where the wild things find their rest,
In resilience they are blessed,
Lessons learned in forest deep,
Promises the trees will keep.

Saga of the Tall Timber

Mighty giants touch the sky,
Centuries have passed them by,
Silent guardians of the land,
Firmly rooted, proudly stand.

Legends carved in bark and wood,
Stories of the ages stood,
Through the years they whisper low,
Tales of life from long ago.

Winter's chill and summer's breeze,
Each one shaped these ancient trees,
Firm and strong they still remain,
Witness to the sun and rain.

Generations come and go,
'Tales these trees alone will know,
Wisdom in their branches spread,
Life and lore in green and red.

In their shadow we find peace,
Time and space in them may cease,
Tall timbers weave a saga grand,
Holding time within their hand.

Standing Through Ages

Through the epochs they have stood,
Witnesses to time and wood,
Silent sentinels of past,
In their presence, shadows cast.

Age-old oaks with gnarled boughs,
Tell of time in timeless vows,
Steadfast through the tempest's rage,
Guardians of a bygone age.

Beneath their leaves the earth does sleep,
Promises that history keep,
Each ring a chapter etched in grain,
In the heart where memories reign.

Century upon century,
Knowledge given to the tree,
In their stillness they bestow,
Wisdom of the earth's long flow.

From their roots deep in the ground,
Silent whispers do resound,
Echoes of an ancient time,
Standing through the ages' climb.

Woodland Sovereignty

In the realm where wildwoods reign,
Nature's kingdom free from chain,
Sovereignty in foliage dressed,
Untamed hearts in green caressed.

Each leaf a sovereign, each tree a king,
Forests' anthem softly sing,
In the courts where shadows meet,
Nature's pulse in rhythm beat.

Verdant crowns reach for the sun,
Declare the rule of all in one,
In the silence of their reign,
Spirits wild and free remain.

Through the grove where legends lie,
Bound by neither earth nor sky,
Ruling with a gentle hand,
Over their unyielding land.

Harmony in roots and sky,
Unified without a cry,
Woodland sovereignty bestowed,
In the peaceful, wild abode.

Witness to Every Dawn

Night’s curtains draw, a sky reborn,
Soft hues of light embrace the morn.
Whispers of dreams slowly recede,
Day’s pure promise, hearts now heed.

Golden fingers stretch and play,
The world awakens, cast away.
Silent sentinels of the dark,
Fade as sparrows sing and lark.

Shadows shrink, light’s steady span,
Welcomes life to wake and plan.
Eyes that glimmer with the spark,
Greeting every day’s embark.

Mountains yawn, rivers gleam,
Night was but a fading dream.
Witness every dawn anew,
Life's perpetual, grand debut.

In the stillness, morning’s grace,
Paints a hope on every face.
Witness to the birth of day,
Dawn renews in gentle sway.

Unyielding Majesty

High above where eagles soar,
Majesty that we adore.
Ancient stone, unmoved, alone,
Silent tales on winds are blown.

Snow-capped peaks and valleys green,
Nature’s grand, eternal scene.
Steadfast as the seasons swing,
In their song, the mountains sing.

Unyielding in their mighty stand,
Lifetimes sculpted by their hand.
Whispered secrets, time’s embrace,
Written on their rugged face.

Majesty of rock and sky,
Silent witness standing by.
To every rise and every fall,
Silent, strong, beholds it all.

Rivers carve, winds softly weep,
Through the ages memories keep.
In their grandeur, find our place,
A humble awe in nature’s grace.

Cycles of the Deep Wood

Under canopies so grand,
Whispers of the ancient land.
Leaves in chorus, wind’s reprise,
Timeless dance beneath the skies.

Seasons pass in quiet flow,
Spring's first bloom to winter's snow.
Cycles of the deep wood's heart,
Nature’s rhythms, fine art.

Silent guardians stand tall,
Witness to life’s rise and fall.
Through the ages, through the change,
In their presence, we arrange.

Rustle of the timeless breeze,
Songs of old among the trees.
Cycles turning, life anew,
Eternal forest, ever true.

Roots deep in the nurturing earth,
Mark the endless circle’s birth.
Cycles of the wood we keep,
In its wisdom, find our sleep.

Branches in Twilight

Setting sun in sky’s embrace,
Paints the world with gentle grace.
Branches in twilight’s soft glow,
Whisper stories of long ago.

Silhouettes in fading light,
Meld with shades of coming night.
Quiet moments, day’s divide,
Nature’s peace in shadows hide.

Every leaf a darker hue,
Promises of night renew.
Branches reach in calm suspense,
Guardians of the night immense.

Stars awaken, dusk’s preview,
Moonlight’s gaze, a silver hue.
In the twilight, branches bend,
Marking time from end to end.

Twilight whispers, light’s refrain,
Embrace of night begins again.
Branches hold the fading day,
Cradling time in gentle sway.

Silent Strength

In silent halls where shadows drift,
A hidden force begins to lift,
Through quiet realms unseen and swift,
Its power subtle, like a gift.

Enduring time, unspoken grace,
It carves its mark in every place,
With gentle hands and patient face,
Silent strength, a firm embrace.

No roar or thunder to proclaim,
No need for echoed, grand acclaim,
Yet mountains bow and skies acclaim,
To silent strength, both wild and tame.

A whisper through the ancient trees,
A ripple on the tranquil seas,
Unseen by all, yet all agrees,
Silent strength moves with the breeze.

So let us honor, soft and true,
The quiet power in skies of blue,
For silent strength, in all we do,
Is ever present, timeless too.

Survivor of Tempests

When tempests rage and skies align,
Against the dark, a flame will shine,
Through brambles thick and walls of pine,
The heart, a beacon, so divine.

With thunderous roars and torrents wild,
The storm may thrash, both fierce and riled,
Yet standing firm, untouched, beguiled,
Survivor smiles, weather compiled.

The wind may howl, the night may tear,
Yet courage breathes the stormy air,
Resilient hearts, beyond compare,
Survivors thrive, their spirits rare.

In battle's wake, amidst the peace,
A strength reborn, the soul's release,
No storm shall claim domain or lease,
Survivor's calm, the noise will cease.

So lift your eyes to skies once gray,
For dawn will break and bring the day,
In every storm, within the fray,
The survivor's light will lead the way.

Nature's Stalwart Keeper

Through forests dense and valleys deep,
A guardian’s vow, the land to keep,
Where shadows dance and secrets sleep,
Nature's keeper’s watch, steadfast and deep.

With ancient wisdom, earth’s delight,
They walk by day and dream by night,
In every leaf and feathered flight,
Their presence known, a guiding light.

In meadows wide and rivers clear,
They hold the wild, forever dear,
With careful hands and vision near,
Nature's keeper stands sincere.

From mountain peaks to ocean's tide,
They honor all the wonders wide,
In every grove and woodland side,
Their spirit walks, a timeless guide.

So let us cherish, wild and free,
Nature's stalwart symphony,
For keepers guard with loyalty,
The earth’s pure heart, for you and me.

Emblem of Persistence

Through trials fierce and roads less worn,
A symbol stands, both weathered, worn,
In every dawn, anew, reborn,
Persistence thrives, a streak of morn.

When shadows fall and hopes are thin,
The emblem glows, a light within,
Against all odds, through thick and thin,
Persistence knows it will begin.

No mountain high, no valley low,
Can halt its steadfast, onward flow,
Through deserts vast and winter's snow,
Persistence grows, a constant glow.

In moments bleak, when faith is small,
It rises up to heed the call,
With every step, to stand, not fall,
Persistence echoes, through it all.

So wear the badge, with heart and soul,
For life's great journey, make it whole,
With every breath, the ultimate goal,
Persistence guides, through all, we stroll.

Milton Keynes UK
Ingram Content Group UK Ltd.
UKHW020330050824
446478UK00015B/496

9 789916 863428